CCSS **Genre** Fiction

Essential Question
How can we protect Earth?

M000238675

Our Beautiful Tree

by Yolanda Garcia
illustrated by George Ulrich

Chapter 1 *Bad News*

"Our treehouse is almost complete!" Jen exclaimed, looking at the tree.

"Yeah! We just need to finish the ladder and it will be done!" said Alex.

Jen and Alex had been working hard on their treehouse. They couldn't wait for it to be finished.

"Let's finish tomorrow. I have to go inside and finish my homework," Alex said.

"Jen! Alex! Time to come inside!" their mother called.

"Mom! Check out our treehouse!" Jen shouted. Mom came out to take a look.

"Doesn't it look great?" Alex added.

"It looks wonderful, kids! But it will get dark soon. You both need to finish your homework before dinner," Mom said.

They settled down at the dining room table. Jen did her math homework. Alex was writing a book report. Everybody was busy as the Sun slowly went down.

Just as Jen and Alex finished up their homework, their mother said, "Please set the table. It is time for dinner."

At dinner, they talked about their day. Jen told her parents she thought she had done well on her math test. Alex said soccer practice had been good that day.

Then their father said, "We have something to tell you."

Alex and Jen were very curious. What was their father going to tell them?

"Our neighbor, Mr. Morris, came by to talk to us today," their father said gently. "He wants us to cut down our tree because the leaves fall into his yard. Then he has to rake them. The small distance between our houses is the problem."

Jen and Alex just looked at their father. They simply could not believe what he was saying to them.

Chapter 2 *Wonderful Memories*

Everybody was very quiet for a moment. "No!" said Jen. "That is our favorite tree. I have loved it ever since I was just a little baby! And now we have our treehouse up there! We have been working so hard on it!" Jen cried.

"Yeah, and the tree is old and beautiful. It helps keep our air clean. It also gives us shade from the sun. Trees are important Earth resources," Alex said.

Everybody had special memories of the tree. They all shared their favorite ones. "I remember when Daddy put up the swing," said Jen. "I could not believe how strong the branch was."

"I can't even imagine how many times I pushed you in that swing," said their father.

Every autumn, Jen and Alex jumped into the enormous piles of colorful leaves.

"One of my favorite memories is how excited you were when the leaves began to fall," said their mother. "You would rake them up and then hop right in!"

"The leaves were such beautiful colors," said Alex. "They were red and orange and yellow."

"I remember the time we had a picnic for the whole neighborhood," said their father. "It was a very hot day. People brought blankets and food. It was nice and cool and shady under the branches."

Everybody agreed that they had rarely had a better time than on that day.

"I don't want to cut down our tree. It's brought us all so many great memories. Something must be done," Mom said.

"I agree. We have to solve this problem," said Alex.

"Yes," said Jen. "We must save our tree!"

Chapter 3 Save Our Tree

The whole family sat at the dining room table and discussed the situation.

"I think if we go and talk to Mr. Morris, we can figure this out," said Dad.

"Well, Mr. Morris can be stubborn sometimes," said Mom. "We will have to figure out exactly what we are going to say to him. We need to have enough information."

The next day, Jen and Alex told all of their friends about the trouble with the tree. Michael thought that it was a good idea to tell Mr. Morris that trees help keep our air clean.

At dinner the family discussed the problem again. "I have another idea!" said Alex. "If Mr. Morris is worried about leaves falling in his yard, I can make a graph showing him when leaves fall. Maybe we can offer to help him rake!"

Everyone agreed that the graph was a good idea and would help convince Mr. Morris to keep the tree.

The next day, the whole family went to visit Mr. Morris. "Mr. Morris, trees are very important," Dad said. "They help keep the air clean. They provide shade on hot days. Also, this tree is very special to our family. If we offer to help rake its leaves, would you consider keeping it?"

Alex handed Mr. Morris his graph. Mr. Morris listened carefully. He was quiet for a moment. Then he said, "I guess if the tree is that important to you all, and I can get some help with raking, the tree can stay."

The tree was saved! Everyone in the neighborhood, even Mr. Morris, came to celebrate.

"We saved our beautiful tree!" said Alex proudly.

"This is the happiest day of my life!" said Jen.

All in all, it was a wonderful day.

Respond to Reading

Summarize

Use important details to help you summarize *Our Beautiful Tree.*

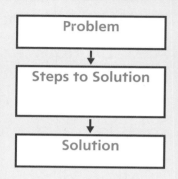

Text Evidence

1. How do you know *Our Beautiful Tree* is fiction? Genre

2. What problem do the characters solve? Tell the steps to the solution. Problem and Solution

3. Use context clues to figure out the meaning of *our* on page 6. Homophones

4. Write about what the family said to Mr. Morris about why the tree should be saved. Write About Reading

DIRT!

Soil might look like dirt to you, but it is one of Earth's most important resources. It is important because it has a supply of things that people and animals need. Soil is mostly little pieces of rock, leaves, and parts of trees. Many insects, like ants, live in the soil. Earthworms do, too.

Earthworms make the soil more useful for everybody.

If there is too much rain, or if it's too hot or too windy, soil can be ruined. That is why it is important to protect soil. One way to do this is by planting. Plants and grass keep soil from washing away or getting too hot. Some farmers plant trees near their fields.

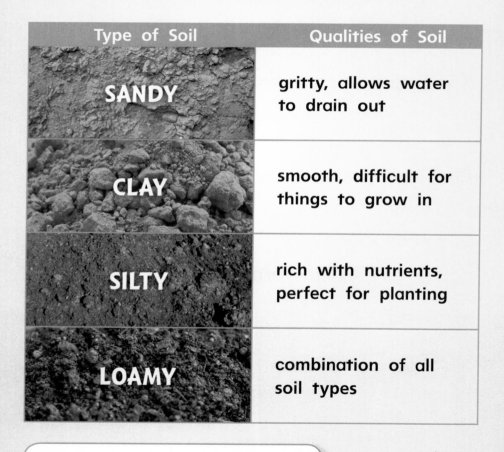

Type of Soil	Qualities of Soil
SANDY	gritty, allows water to drain out
CLAY	smooth, difficult for things to grow in
SILTY	rich with nutrients, perfect for planting
LOAMY	combination of all soil types

There are many types of soil.

Many things that you eat every day come from soil. Carrots and potatoes grow under the soil. Other vegetables, such as green beans, grow on plants in the soil. So do fruits. Melons grow on vines that are on the ground. Dirt is very important to everybody!

Tomatoes need soil to grow, too.

Make Connections
How do farmers help to protect Earth? **Essential Question**

Why is it important to protect trees and soil? Text to Text

Focus on
Science

Purpose To find out ways to help the environment

What to Do

Step 1 With a partner, brainstorm how you can help the environment and save Earth.

Step 2 Make a list of all of the things you can do.

Step 3 Using your list, make a poster of your favorite ideas.

Conclusion Share your poster with your family. Ask your family to try your ideas.